Queen Elizabeth I: 60 For Kids

by Vanessa Ellis

All Rights Reserved. Published by "Fascinating Facts For Kids". No part of this publication may be reproduced in any form or by any means, including scanning, photocopying, or otherwise without prior written permission of the copyright holder. Copyright Vanessa Ellis © 2015

This book is just one of a series of "Fascinating Facts For Kids" books. For more fascinating facts about people, history, animals and more please visit:

www.fascinatingfactsforkids.com

Contents

Introduction..1

Early Life...4

Henry's Death and a New Queen.........7

Elizabeth Becomes Queen................... 10

Elizabeth Says "No" to Marriage.........12

Mary, Queen of Scots..........................13

The Spanish Armada.......................... 15

The Golden Age.................................. 20

Rebellion..24

Elizabeth's Death................................26

Conclusion.. 28

Introduction

The Tudors, the famous noble family of the 16th century, gave us two of the most famous monarchs ever to rule England, Henry VIII and his daughter Elizabeth I. Elizabeth was Queen of England for 44 years during what some call the "Golden Age".

Henry VIII

Elizabeth was Queen in a man's world and won respect for her intelligence, wisdom and charm. She had her faults though - she could be bad-tempered and often found it difficult to reach a decision, but she remains one of the greatest rulers that England has had.

Elizabeth I

She ruled in difficult and dangerous times, often being at war with Spain and France, but England became a powerful and prosperous country during her reign. She sent her sailors on daring missions to explore the world, saw the blossoming of English art and music and she established the Church of England after the country had separated from the Roman Catholic Church during her father's reign.

We hope the following facts will fascinate you and encourage you to find out more about Queen Elizabeth I.

Early Life

1. Elizabeth Tudor was born on September 7, 1533, at Greenwich Palace, the only child of King Henry VIII and his second wife, Anne Boleyn.

Greenwich Palace

2. At the time of her birth, Elizabeth was heir to the throne of England, although her father Henry was desperate for a son to succeed him as King.

3. Elizabeth had an older half-sister, Mary, who was Henry's daughter from his first marriage. Mary had been stripped of her title of Princess and was angry that Elizabeth would be the next Queen instead of her.

4. Henry was certain that Anne Boleyn would not give him the son he wanted and was determined to get rid of her so that he could marry again. He accused her of crimes she didn't commit and had her beheaded.

Anne Boleyn

5. Henry was now able to marry Jane Seymour, whom he had fallen in love with, and she soon gave birth to Edward, the boy that the King had so desperately wanted. Henry was overjoyed that he now had a son as heir to the throne.

6. King Henry made sure that his children were well educated. Elizabeth loved learning and was a talented pupil. She learned many languages and studied science, philosophy, theology, music and ancient history, growing up into an intelligent and elegant young woman.

Henry's Death and a New Queen

7. Towards the end of his reign, King Henry became ill and made a will declaring that if Edward were to have no children before he died then Mary would be crowned and if Mary were to die childless then Elizabeth would become Queen.

8. Henry died on January 28, 1547, and the nine-year-old Edward became King of England.

9. Edward, who was a sickly child, died in 1553 at the age of 15. Before his death he had decided that his cousin, Lady Jane Grey, was to be his successor. She was horrified that she was forced to be crowned Queen as she knew that Mary was the rightful heir to the throne.

10. Mary was angry that she was not to be the Queen as her father had wished and assembled an army against Lady Jane Grey, who ruled for just nine days before Mary had her beheaded.

11. Mary was crowned in July, 1553, and married a fellow Catholic, Prince Philip of Spain.

12. During Henry VIII's reign, England was a Roman Catholic Country. When he wanted to end his first marriage Henry had to get permission from the Pope, who was head of the Catholic Church. When the Pope refused, Henry divorced his wife anyway and started an English, Protestant church. From then on there was mistrust between Protestants and Catholics in England.

Philip of Spain

13. Mary was determined that England would be Catholic again and anyone who disagreed would run the risk of being burned at the stake. During her reign, Mary had nearly 300 people put to death in this way, earning her the nickname of "Bloody Mary".

14. The Catholic Mary did not trust her Protestant half-sister whom she believed was plotting against her and Elizabeth was imprisoned in the Tower of London.

The Tower of London

15. Elizabeth was eventually released from prison, but Mary was still suspicious and had her confined to a house in Oxfordshire where she could be watched closely.

Elizabeth Becomes Queen

16. Mary reigned for five years before dying childless on November 17, 1558, and Elizabeth became Queen of England at the age of 25. She came to the throne at a difficult and dangerous time and would have many important decisions to make.

17. Women at the time were looked upon as weak and inferior to men, but Elizabeth was convinced that God had chosen her to become Queen and she had no feelings of inadequacy.

18. Elizabeth's coronation took place at Westminster Abbey on January 15, 1559, and was followed by a great banquet at Westminster Hall.

Westminster Abbey

19. Although not passionately religious, Elizabeth was a Protestant and took over a country which was divided between Protestants and Catholics. Many thought that the Queen's cousin, the Catholic Mary Stuart, should have become Queen of England instead of Elizabeth in order to restore the Catholic faith to the country.

20. Elizabeth ordered all her subjects to become Protestants, but unlike Mary she did not have people who refused burned alive. She was more interested in loyalty to the crown than a person's religious beliefs.

21. Elizabeth had a group of advisors, the Privy Council, to help with important decisions but she expected to get her own way and often ignored their advice. Members of the Privy Council included such eminent men as William Cecil, Lord Burghley and Sir Francis Walsingham.

22. William Cecil was the most important member of the Privy Council, holding the title of Secretary of State. He joined the Council at the age of 38 and served in it until the day he died 40 years later.

23. The Privy Council still meets today and is made up mostly of senior politicians who advise the present-day Queen, although it does not have the power and influence that it had in the time of Elizabeth I.

Elizabeth Says "No" to Marriage

24. It was expected that the new Queen would marry in order to produce an heir to the throne and many Kings and Princes from all over Europe were keen to marry Elizabeth.

25. In those days, royalty didn't marry for love, but for power. If a King and Queen from different countries were married, then their countries would be united.

26. But Elizabeth had no interest in marriage, motherhood or handing over much of her power to a foreigner. She had also seen how her father had treated his own wives, including having her own mother executed.

Mary, Queen of Scots

27. In 1543, Elizabeth's cousin, Mary Stuart, became Queen of Scotland when she was just six days old. Being a great-niece of Henry VIII she had a claim to the English throne and when Queen Mary of England died many English Catholics, as well as Catholics across Europe, would have preferred her as the Queen rather than the Protestant Elizabeth.

Mary, Queen of Scots

28. Mary spent most of her childhood in France before returning to Scotland in 1561. She had many difficulties ruling over Scotland and was forced to leave the country in 1568. Mary fled to

England where she asked Elizabeth for protection.

29. Elizabeth allowed her cousin to stay in England even though it was thought that she and her supporters were planning on taking the English crown.

30. Mary was spied on for nearly 20 years, until, in 1586, evidence was found that Mary was indeed plotting against Elizabeth. Mary was put on trial and found guilty of treason, for which the punishment was death.

31. Elizabeth reluctantly signed her cousin's death warrant and Mary was beheaded in February, 1587, at Fotheringay Castle in Northamptonshire.

The Spanish Armada

32. Philip of Spain, a fellow Catholic like Mary, was furious that Elizabeth had put to death a Catholic Queen and he declared war on England.

33. An Armada, which was a fleet of Spanish warships, was launched with the aims of invading England, putting Philip on the English throne and converting the country back to the Catholic faith.

34. The English were ready for the Spanish attack, having spent months building ships for the navy and assembling a huge army.

35. Part of the English navy was stationed at Plymouth, the first sea-port the Spanish would encounter on their journey from Spain. The rest was sent to Dover at the other end of the English Channel.

36. 20,000 men were placed along the southern coast of England to repel any attempt at invasion and London was protected by troops stationed near the mouth of the River Thames at Tilbury.

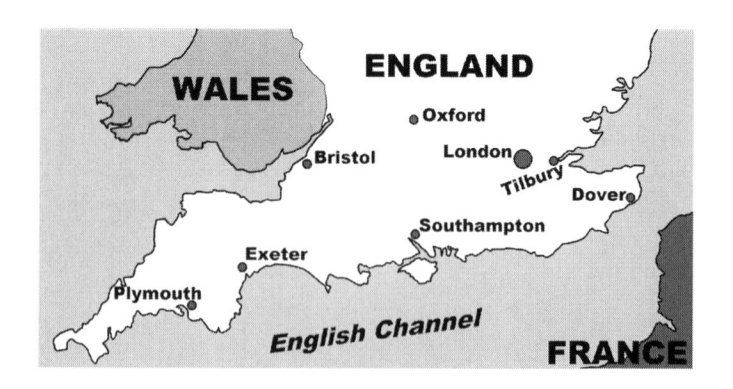

The Southern Coast of England

37.   Elizabeth visited the army guarding London, riding on horseback and dressed like a soldier.

38.   She gave a rousing speech to her men and declared that she would join in the fighting should the Spanish land on English soil. Some of her words were, "I have, I know, only the body of a weak and feeble woman, but I have the heart and stomach of a King, and of a King of England too, and I am ready for my God, my Kingdom and my people, to have that body laid down, even in the dust. If the battle comes, therefore, I shall myself be in the midst and front of it, to live or die with you".

39.   The massive Armada eventually came into sight from the English shore, 130 ships stretching out for seven miles, and it made its way along the English Channel towards London.

The Spanish Armada

40. The large, cumbersome Spanish galleons were attacked by the smaller, quicker English ships, watched from the shore by thousands of onlookers. One Spanish ship after another was taken or destroyed by the English, so that by the time the Armada reached Dover it was in complete disarray.

41. The Spanish did not dare head back to Spain the way they had come, instead making the long and dangerous voyage around the coast of Scotland and the west coast of Ireland where more ships were lost. Less than half the fleet made it back to Spain and the invasion of England was thwarted.

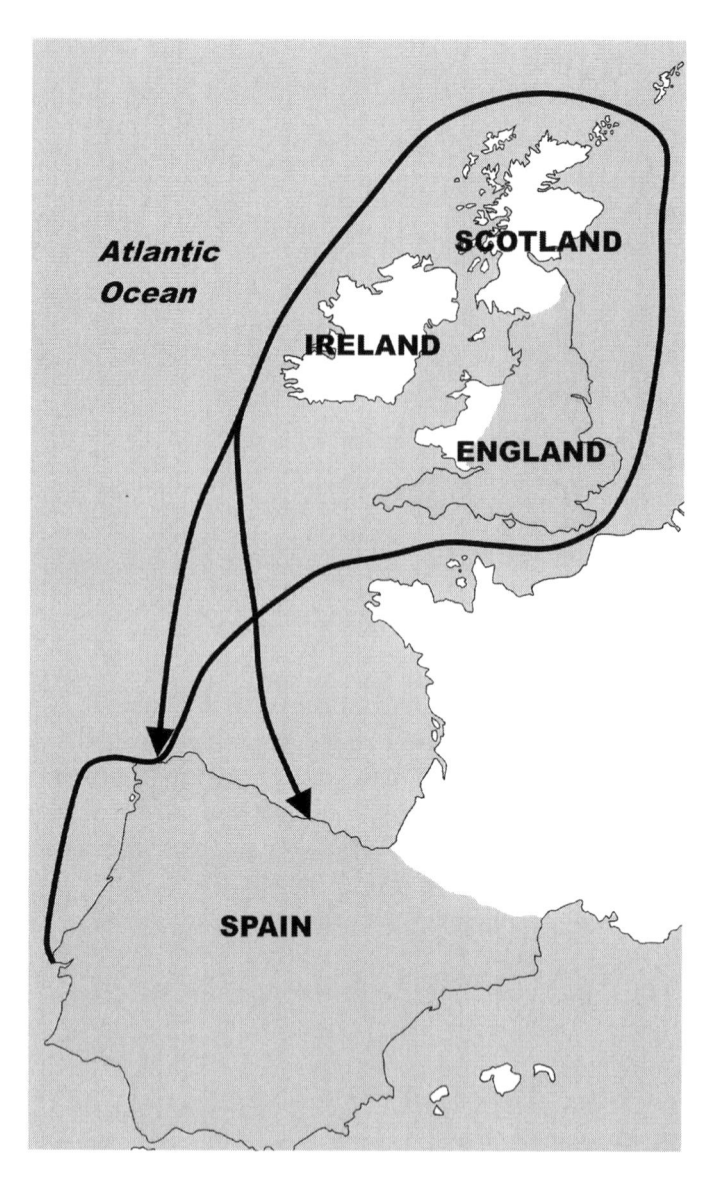

The Route of the Spanish Armada

42. There were celebrations across all of England after the defeat of the Armada. Bonfires were lit, church bells rang out and there was a Thanksgiving Service at St. Paul's Cathedral. The defeat of the powerful Spanish Armada had laid the foundations for England's naval supremacy on the seas in later years.

The Golden Age

43. Elizabeth was now at the height of her powers and adored by her subjects. She ruled over a country that was confident and optimistic.

44. The Elizabethan age was a time of great exploration as men such as Sir Francis Drake and Sir Walter Raleigh crossed the Atlantic to claim lands in the "New World" of America for their Queen.

45. Drake became the first Englishman to sail round the world in his ship, 'Golden Hind'. On this epic three-year voyage he plundered many ports of the Spanish Empire on the west coast of America. He returned home to England with a great deal of Spanish treasure and many spices from foreign lands. He had become a national hero and was knighted by Queen Elizabeth for his exploits.

Drake's Route Around the World

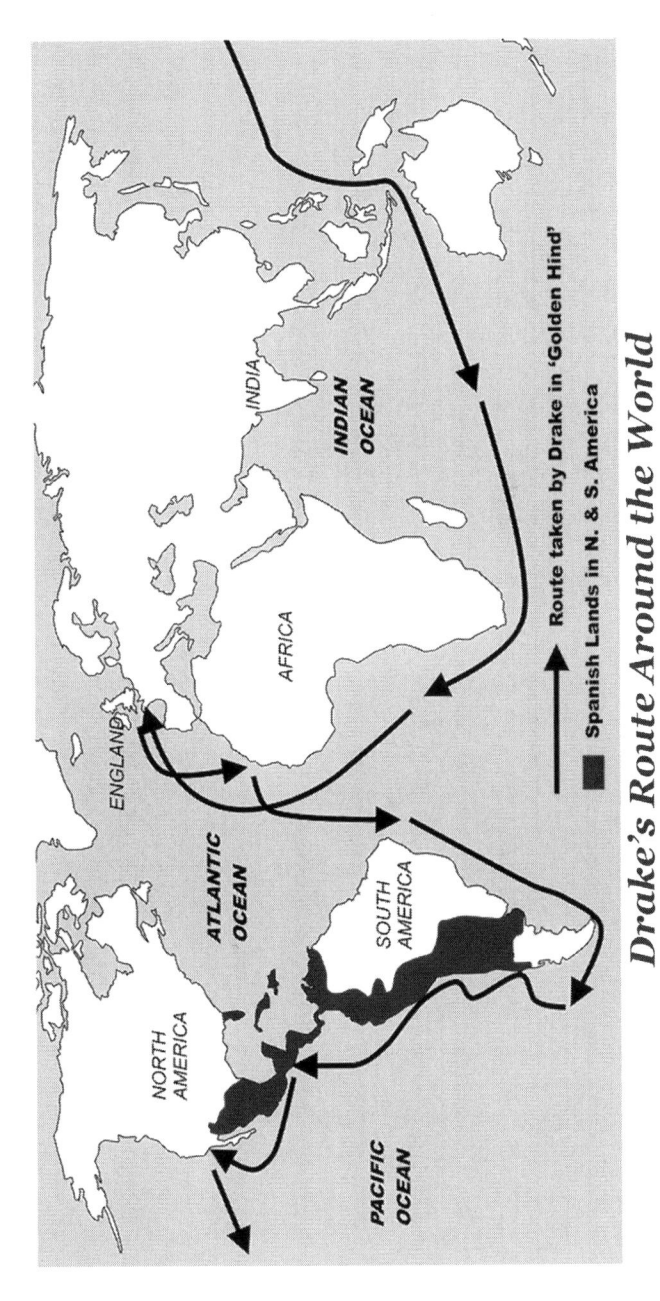

46. Music flourished during this "Golden Age" with composers such as William Byrd, John Dowland and Thomas Tallis establishing an English school of music. Elizabeth was a keen musician and music and dancing played a big part in life at her court. She employed her own orchestra which comprised of about 30 musicians.

47. The theatre also thrived during Elizabeth's reign, producing playwrights such as Ben Jonson, Christopher Marlowe and the greatest of them all, William Shakespeare. Queen Elizabeth regularly attended performances of Shakespeare's plays which appealed to people from all levels of society.

William Shakespeare

48. Elizabeth liked to meet her subjects as often as possible and during the summer months she would take her whole court away from London to visit other parts of the country.

49. Elizabeth's court didn't look forward to these visits as it was very tiring being constantly on the move and although the Queen was looked after very well by her hosts, the same could not be said of others.

50. Elizabeth chose to stay at the great houses and castles of nobleman in different parts of the country during these visits. They did not always look forward to accommodating and entertaining so many people though, as it was very expensive! The Queen would often decide to stay for many days and the costs to the host could run into hundreds of pounds, which in those days was a great deal of money!

51. When visiting new towns, Elizabeth often had to sit through endless speeches by the local politicians, but if she was ever bored by this, her good manners wouldn't let her show it! What was important to her was to be in contact with the English people and her subjects appreciated this.

Rebellion

52.   Towards the end of her reign, Elizabeth became close to the Earl of Essex, a handsome and ambitious young nobleman.

Robert Devereux, 2nd Earl of Essex

53.   The Queen and Essex often quarrelled and during one of these disagreements the Queen finally lost patience with Essex's behavior and the friendship was over.

54. Essex resented the way he had been treated and convinced himself that Elizabeth was not ruling wisely. He decided that he had to get rid of her so that he could take over the running of the country. He found some support for his plan, but most people were loyal to Elizabeth.

55. Elizabeth's spies found out about Essex's plot and he was arrested and tried for treason. On being found guilty he was sentenced to death and executed in February, 1601, at the Tower of London. He was the last person to be beheaded there.

56. Despite Essex's treachery, Elizabeth became depressed by his death and her health was affected.

Elizabeth's Death

57. Elizabeth was nearly 70 years old by now and as her health worsened, the end of her life seemed to be approaching. The question of who would rule after her had to be answered.

58. As Elizabeth had not married or had children, she had to name her successor. She had not done this earlier because she feared that if she did, it could cause problems as it had done with her and her half-sister, Queen Mary.

59. In March, 1603, as death approached, she finally chose the next ruler of England. It was to be King James VI of Scotland, who was the son of her old enemy, Mary Stuart. As King of England and Scotland, the crowning of James was the first attempt at uniting the two countries, which eventually happened in 1707.

60. On March 24, 1603, Elizabeth died at Richmond Palace at the age of 69. After an elaborate and magnificent funeral she was buried in Westminster Abbey, the place where she was crowned 44 years ago.

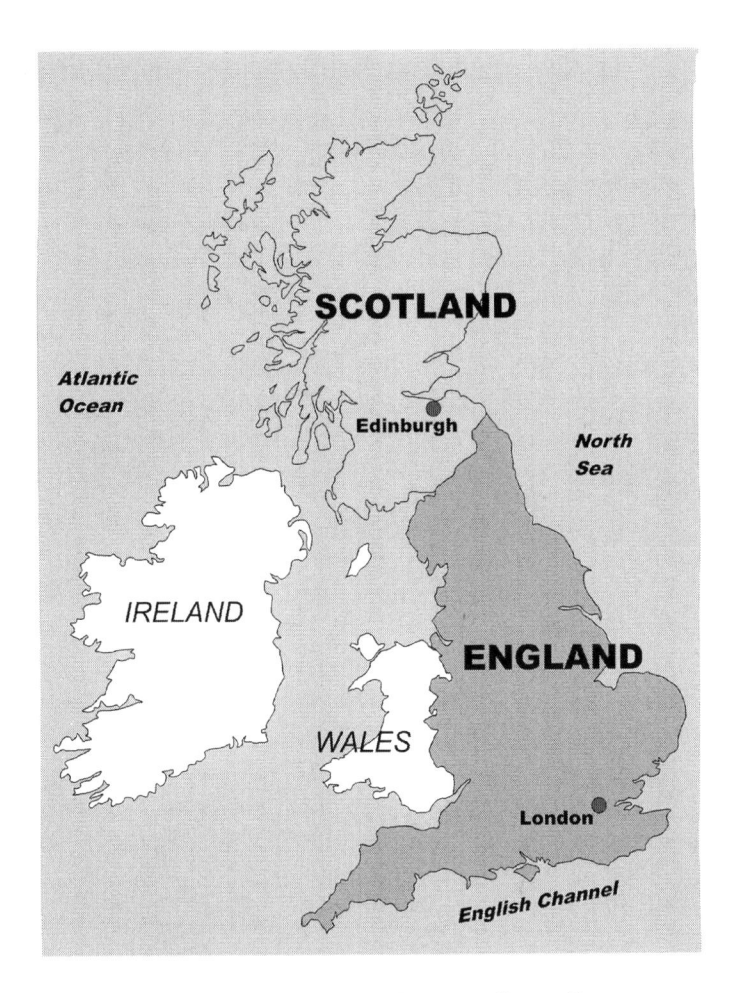

England and Scotland

Conclusion

As Elizabeth had no children, she was the last member of the Tudor family to rule over England. But with the choice of James as the new King of England, Elizabeth had united Scotland and England for the first time.

The achievements during Elizabeth's reign were remarkable. The colonies and trading posts that were founded overseas marked the beginning of the British Empire, one of the most powerful empires in history.

The establishment of the Church of England and the defeat of the Spanish Armada had brought great pride to the people of England, who enjoyed a prosperity and stability that they had not known before.

The Elizabethan Era was a "Golden Age" for art, music, poetry and theatre, as England became an important European cultural centre.

By the end of her long reign, Elizabeth had become perhaps the most loved, popular and successful monarch in the history of England.

For more in the Fascinating Facts For Kids series, please visit:

www.fascinatingfactsforkids.com

Printed in Great Britain
by Amazon.co.uk, Ltd.,
Marston Gate.